Glasgow and Dunbartonshire's Lo

by
Gordon Stansfield

Class 4 2-6-4T No. 42173 passes Eglinton Street Station with the 7.50 p.m. service from Glasgow Central to Lanark, 9 June 1954.

Text © Gordon Stansfield, 2003.
First published in the United Kingdom, 2003,
by Stenlake Publishing,
Telephone / Fax: 01290 551122

ISBN 1 84033 235 2

The publishers wish to thank the following for contributing photographs to this book: Hugh Brodie for the inside front cover and pages 5 and 39; Neville Stead for page 21; Neville Stead and P.B. Booth for page 37; Neville Stead and G.M. Staddon for pages 16, 27 and 28; D.E. Shepherd for page 23; and W.A.C. Smith for pages 1–3, 8–13, 15, 17–20, 22, 24–26, 29, 32 upper, 34, 35, 38, 40–48, the inside back cover and the back cover.

The 7.07 p.m. diesel multiple unit from Craigendoran to Arrochar and Tarbet Station arrives at Rhu on 30 May 1964.

INTRODUCTION

Glasgow is unique among British cities in that it has the largest rail network outside of London. Instead of services declining, the opposite has occurred with services being reinstated on lines such as those between Glasgow and Maryhill and Whifflet and Cumbernauld, with the possibility of more in future years.

The industrial age of the late nineteenth century required good rail services, not just for freight but also for passengers. The railway companies of the day envisaged great potential for growth and even went as far as offering free rail seasons to induce affluent citizens to buy houses in what was then the leafy suburb of Lenzie. Competition between rival companies was rife. For example, the North British and the Caledonian vied for traffic westwards from Glasgow towards Clydebank and Dumbarton on different lines which ran very close to each other, with some stations even having the same name. These companies took immense pride in their city centre terminals. Glasgow boasted four, of which only two remain – Queen Street and Central. The Glasgow and South Western Railway Company operated from St Enoch Station to destinations in Ayrshire and Renfrewshire while the Caledonian ran into Lanarkshire and Dunbartonshire from Central Station. In addition, the Caledonian operated from Buchanan Street to serve destinations mainly north of Perth. Finally, the North British operated out of Queen Street to Dunbartonshire and Stirlingshire.

The expansion of tram services and, latterly, bus services had a profound effect on Glasgow's suburban routes in the twentieth century. Tram and bus fares were not only cheaper but services were more frequent. As most of Glasgow's suburban services ran through tunnels, travelling by steam train was not an enjoyable experience. In an attempt to keep themselves free of soot and grime many passengers carried paper bags in order to open carriage doors. The result of all this was some early closures such as Botanic Gardens and Kirklee stations.

With the decline of major manufacturing industries in the 1950s and '60s passenger levels fell and closures took place. However, in 1960 there was a major revitalisation of services with the introduction of the 'Blue Trains', so called by Glaswegians because of their blue colour. These electric trains provided a fast, clean and efficient service for work and play and brought back passengers in their thousands to the rail network.

It is hoped that this book will not only rekindle fond memories of days gone by, but will also show just how important a role railways played in Glasgow and Dunbartonshire. There is even a mention of the revolutionary monorail prototype designed by George Bennie and operated near Milngavie. Kirkintilloch and the surrounding area is also included for at one time this formed part of Dunbartonshire.

At Buchanan Street Station on 31 August 1965, B4 Pacific No. 60026, 'Miles Beevor', heads the 5.30 p.m. express for Aberdeen while B1 No. 61244, 'Strang Steel', heads the 5.35 p.m. to Dunblane.

Aberfoyle – Kirkintilloch *

Passenger service withdrawn	1 October 1951
Distance	26.25 miles
Company	North British

* Closed stations on this line that were in Perthshire were Aberfoyle and Gartmore. Closed stations in Stirlingshire were Buchlyvie, Balfron, Killearn, Dumgoyne, Blanefield, Strathblane, Campsie Glen, Lennoxtown (Blane Valley), Lennoxtown and Milton of Campsie.

Known as the Blane Valley Railway, this single track rail line rambled its way through the area known as the Blane Valley which lies at the foot of the Campsie hills, covering the terrain between Blanefield and Aberfoyle. Opened in several sections over a period of about thirty years, the southern section of the line continued beyond Kirkintilloch to Lenzie to join the main Glasgow to Edinburgh route (see the Kirkintilloch – Lenzie section for details). The first section opened to passengers ran from Lenzie to Lennoxtown, but it was not until July 1867 that the line was extended westwards to reach Dumgoyne before finally arriving at Aberfoyle in October 1882. This line traversed three counties: in Dunbartonshire it reached to just beyond Kirkintilloch, in Stirlingshire to near Gartmore, and in Perthshire to Aberfoyle. Trains were few and far between, most originating from Glasgow Queen Street High Level Station. The rail route was much longer that the same journey by road and in latter years the services tended to be provided by a steam railcar.

The bridge just beyond Anniesland Station. Both are still open.

Anniesland (Knightswood South Junction) – Maryhill (Maryhill Park Junction)

Passenger service withdrawn	2 April 1951	Company	North British
Distance	1.25 miles		

This short spur in Glasgow's west end linked Anniesland Station, on the present day north suburban electric service to Helensburgh and Balloch, with Maryhill Park Station which today forms the western terminus of the diesel service from Glasgow Queen Street High level to Maryhill. This route never saw a regular passenger service apart from infrequent journeys from Kilsyth and Torrance to Queen Street Low Level which ended in 1951. However, the line formed part of a circle round Glasgow which allowed empty passenger rolling stock movements to take place for services arriving at Queen Street Low Level. The line also carried workers' trains from areas such as Clydebank and the Clydeside shipyards to Springburn and the east of the city without having to go via the city centre. These services continued until 1959. The main traffic over the Anniesland to Maryhill line was freight but this ended in 1980. Strathclyde Passenger Transport Executive saw a potential use for this short line and intended to use it as the western terminus of a new Maryhill service. This would have enabled a service to run from Queen Street High level to Anniesland which would have then become an interchange station. Although the track bed was retained, including a bay platform at Anniesland, this project never came to fruition. When the Maryhill service was introduced in December 1993 with the reopening of several new stations, in addition to the reopening of Maryhill Park Station which was renamed Maryhill, the trains used the same line as West Highland trains to Oban and Fort William. Trains terminate at Maryhill Station, although they run empty to just outside Westerton Station before making a return journey (see the Westerton – Cowlairs section for details).

Balloch (Forth and Clyde Junction) – Gartness (Gartness Junction) *

Passenger service withdrawn	1 October 1934	*Stations closed*	*Date*
Distance	8.75 miles	Jamestown	1 October 1934
Company	North British	Caldarvan	1 October 1934

Jamestown Station.

This line was part of the route from Balloch to Stirling. Opened in 1856 by the Forth and Clyde Railway, it was envisaged as a trunk route from the central belt to the west of Scotland, although in the end it remained essentially rural. In the final few years prior to closure Sentinel railcars operated the service from Balloch to Stirling, but patronage was limited. The original viaduct which the line used to cross the River Leven between Balloch and Jamestown can still be viewed today as it forms a pedestrian walkway.

* The closed stations on this line that were in Stirlingshire were Drymen and Gartness.

Balloch Pier – Balloch Central

Passenger service withdrawn	28 September 1986	*Station closed*	*Date*
Distance	0.5 miles	Balloch Pier	28 September 1986
Company	Dumbarton and Balloch		

Situated at the southern end of Loch Lomond, Balloch Pier Station was adjacent to the pier from which services and cruises to Balmaha, Rowardennan, Luss and Inversnaid departed. Train services, which began about 1850, connected with the loch sailings and through trains from most areas of Glasgow ran to the pier station. Rivalry between the railway companies was very intense, although none of the major ones owned the line from Dumbarton to Balloch. Instead it was a small company, the Dumbarton and Balloch Railway, which allowed the Caledonian and North British railway companies to operate train services over the line, from Glasgow Central and Glasgow Queen Street Low Level stations respectively. When the Glasgow north suburban services were electrified in 1960 with the introduction of the 'Blue Trains', the route to Balloch Pier saw an increase in day trippers to Loch Lomond. The most famous steamer on the loch was the *Maid of the Loch*, its claim to fame being that it was the only paddle steamer in the world which operated on an inland loch. After the *Maid* was withdrawn from service in the 1980s due to high running costs and a drop in passenger numbers, a smaller ship, *Countess Fiona*, provided a service although this too was withdrawn after several summer seasons. However, the *Maid* may return to service within the next few years and it can now be viewed at Balloch Pier as it undergoes restoration. The track bed from the pier station to Balloch Central, which was closed in April 1988 and – renamed as Balloch – relocated to the other side of a level crossing, is still visible today along with the original station buildings which are used by the local tourist information office.

Bowling (Dunglass Junction) – Rutherglen (North Junction)

Passenger service withdrawn	5 October 1964	*Stations closed*	*Date*
Distance	13.75 miles	Bowling	5 February 1951
Company	Caledonian	Old Kilpatrick	5 October 1964
		Dalmuir Riverside	5 October 1964
		Kilbowie	5 October 1964

Bowling Station.

Stations closed	Date	Stations closed	Date
Clydebank Riverside	5 October 1964	Anderston Cross **	3 August 1959
Yoker Ferry	5 October 1964	Glasgow Central Low Level ***	5 October 1964
Scotstoun West	5 October 1964	Glasgow Cross	5 October 1964
Scotstoun East	5 October 1964	Glasgow Green	2 November 1953
Whiteinch Riverside	5 October 1964	Bridgeton Cross ****	5 October 1964
Kelvin Hall	5 October 1964	Dalmarnock (first station)	1 November 1895
Stobcross *	3 September 1959	Dalmarnock ***	5 October 1964

Old Kilpatrick Station.

* Reopened 5 November 1979 and renamed Finnieston. Renamed Exhibition Centre in 1986.
** Reopened 5 November 1979 and renamed Anderston.

*** Reopened 5 November 1979.
**** Reopened 5 November 1979 and renamed Bridgeton.

Dalmuir Riverside Station on its day of closure. Class 4 2-6-0 No. 76074 heads the last train at 12.05 p.m., a service to Rutherglen.

This route was created by the Caledonian Railway to compete directly with the North British Railway Company who had many lines and stations in the same area. The western part of the line, from Dumbarton Central to Bowling, is still in use today as part of the North Clyde Electric Suburban services. Having crossed the Forth and Clyde Canal, the line ran fairly close to the Clyde shoreline for much of its length. It served several shipyards and associated works, and there were numerous branches to other lines which allowed a high volume of freight and passenger traffic to be carried.

Homeward-bound workers from John Brown's shipyard join the 4.26 p.m. train from Balloch to Rutherglen, hauled by class 3 2-6-2T No. 40188, at Clydebank Riverside Station on 4 April 1958.

When the line first opened to passenger traffic in 1896, Glasgow Central Low Level Station saw 260 train arrivals and departures each weekday. The decline in heavy industry, along with population movement, led to a considerable decline in passenger usage of the line and towards the end of its life most trains were provided for workers engaged at the various works along the line.

Class 4 2-6-4T No. 42058 at Yoker Ferry Station with the 5.16 p.m. service from Dalmuir Riverside to Rutherglen on 25 September 1964.

Although the line closed in 1964, it was reopened in part in November 1979 as the Argyle line. A spur was built between the new station of Partick (which replaced Partick Hill Station) and Stobcross which joined the remaining section towards Glasgow Central and Rutherglen. In the west, part of the former line has been converted into the Loch Lomond Cycleway which links Glasgow and Balloch.

Black Five No. 45155 at Whiteinch Riverside Station with a 9.00 a.m. excursion from Dalmuir Riverside to Leven on Easter Monday, 22 April 1957.

Many stations along this line had the same name as their North British counterparts and it was inevitable that name changes would have to come about under British Railways in order to avoid confusion. Some names were changed much earlier. Just four years after the line was opened Scotstoun Station was renamed Scotstoun West and Victoria Park was renamed Scotstoun East. Kilbowie Road Station was renamed Kilbowie at the same time. In May 1952 Dalmuir had its name changed to Dalmuir Riverside and on 28 February 1953 Whiteinch became Whiteinch Riverside. In July of the same year Yoker had its name changed to Yoker Ferry. The last name change took place in June 1959 when Partick Central was renamed Kelvin Hall. During the First World War, and afterwards for short periods, some stations were closed due to manpower shortages including Bowling and Glasgow Green.

Black Five No. 45169 at Kelvin Hall Station, awaiting departure with a special train returning to Dumfries from the Scottish Industries Exhibition on 17 September 1959.

Class 4 2-6-4T No. 4220 arrives at Stobcross Station with the 5.15 p.m. service from Balloch to Rutherglen on 23 July 1959.

Glasgow Cross Station, on the left, c.1902.

Class N15 0-6-2T No. 69163 at the closed Glasgow Green Station with a Branch Line Society railtour from Maryhill, 6 May 1961.

Locomotive No. 67487 at Bridgeton Cross Station on 14 August 1954.

Bridgeton – High Street (High Street Junction)

Passenger service withdrawn	5 November 1979	*Stations closed*	*Date*
Distance	1 mile	Bridgeton *	5 November 1979
Company	North British	Gallowgate Central	1917

On 10 July 1955 class VI 2-6-2T No. 67643 waits to leave Bridgeton Central Station with the Sunday 5.45 p.m. service to Helensburgh. On the left No. 67678 is on empty stock.

This line opened on 1 June 1892. Bridgeton was one of the North British Railway's Glasgow city terminuses and many suburban services to the north-west of the city – such as to Milngavie, Balloch and Helensburgh – operated from there. With the introduction of the 'blue trains' in 1960 the line was electrified and continued in use until the Argyle line opened in November 1979. This involved the reopening of Bridgeton Station on the Glasgow Central Low Level line. Following closure the station became Bridgeton Central Carriage Depot, a stabling point for rolling stock which continued in use until June 1987 when the extensive depot at Yoker was opened. Bridgeton Station had about six platforms and was demolished in the 1990s with no trace remaining.   * Originally known as Bridgeton Cross; known as Bridgeton Central from January 1954 and then as Bridgeton from June 1965.

Bridgeton Cross – Newton

Passenger service withdrawn	5 October 1964	*Stations closed*	*Date*
Distance	6.5 miles	Parkhead Stadium *	5 October 1964
Company	Caledonian	Tollcross	5 October 1964
		Carmyle	5 October 1964

Class 3 2-6-2T No. 40176 at Parkhead Stadium Station with a 4.50 p.m. return football special to Possil on 4 October 1958.

This line left the Glasgow Central Low Level line at Bridgeton Cross before travelling south-east to reach Carmyle Station where it joined the Rutherglen to Coatbridge route. The route never carried a regular passenger service until 1933 when a frequent service was introduced from Glasgow Central to Whifflet which involved the reopening of Carmyle Station. After leaving Carmyle the Newton line crossed the River Clyde and there was a junction which allowed some trains to reach Kirkhill. There were no intermediate stations between Carmyle and Newton. Most of the services which called at Parkhead Stadium and Tollcross ran from Glasgow Central Low Level to Coatbridge. The Newton services were always very sparse – even in 1922 there were only four trains in each direction Monday to Saturday. Before closure only one train used the section from Carmyle to Newton and this was an early morning steam train from Glasgow Central Low Level to Shotts. The line remained in use for freight traffic from Carmyle to Westburn Steel Works until 30 May 1983.

* Known as Parkhead until 3 March 1952.

Buchanan Street – Sighthill East Junction

Passenger service withdrawn	7 November 1966	*Stations closed*	*Date*
Distance	2 miles	Buchanan Street	7 November 1966
Company	Caledonian	Townhead	1 November 1849
		St Rollox	5 November 1962

Standard class 5 No. 73152 leaves Buchanan Street Station on 29 October 1965 with the 1315 service to Dundee Tay Bridge.

Class 4 2-6-4T No. 42275 at St Rollox Station with the 4.12 p.m. from Buchanan Street to Hamilton on 20 April 1962.

Buchanan Street Station was the Glasgow terminus for services to Aberdeen, Stirling, Perth, Dundee, Crieff, Inverness and Oban. Opened to passengers on 1 November 1849, the line required extensive engineering works before reaching Buchanan Street (the original terminus had been Townhead Station, outside the city centre). Tunnels under St Rollox and the Forth and Clyde Canal had to be built, as did deep cuttings. In line with the other Glasgow termini – Central, St Enoch and Queen Street – the Caledonian wanted to build a station hotel, but despite approval being given this was never built. Buchanan Street never became as grand as the other Glasgow stations. It only had five platforms and suffered from cramped buildings and facilities. Although the London Midland and Scottish Railway Company did carry out some improvements in the late 1920s, it remained the poor relation of the other three city centre stations. At one time British Rail's Scottish headquarters occupied the station site with building work starting before the station was closed. All services which used Buchanan Street were diverted to Queen Street Station. St Rollox Station, which opened in August 1883, served the large locomotive works of the same name.

Clydebank East – Yoker (Clydebank East Junction)

Passenger service withdrawn	14 September 1959	*Station closed*	*Date*
Distance	0.75 miles	Clydebank East	14 September 1959
Company	North British		

Clydebank East Station.

The station at Clydebank East was the original terminus of the Glasgow, Yoker and Clydebank Railway before it was taken over by the North British Railway. An Act of Parliament of 1893 resulted in the line being extended from Clydebank to Dalmuir and when the new line opened in May 1897 Clydebank Station was renamed Clydebank East and a new station called Clydebank Central (the present-day Clydebank Station) was opened. Clydebank East was one of several stations all located within about a mile of each other in the town. The two which remain in use today are Singer and Clydebank, but there were others at Kilbowie Road, Clydebank Riverside and Singer Works Platform. These were required because of the large daily influx of workers to the shipyards and the works of the Singer Sewing Machine Company. Numerous trains arrived each morning from as far afield as Airdrie in the east and Balloch in the west. Clydebank East lasted until the late 1950s with an irregular service to Glasgow Queen Street Low Level and beyond. In that decade the latter station hosted the departure of what were known as 'Starlight Specials' to London which offered overnight cheap fares to the capital.

Craigendoran Pier – Craigendoran Junction

Passenger service withdrawn	25 September 1972	Station closed	Date
Distance	0.25 miles	Craigendoran Pier	25 September 1972
Company	North British		

Class C15 4-4-2T No. 67460 at Craigendoran Pier Station with the 7.00 p.m. push/pull to Arrochar and Tarbet, 1 June 1957.

Craigendoran Pier Station came into use in 1882 after the North British Railway realised that Helensburgh was an unsuitable location for basing its steamer services. Like the Caledonian and Glasgow and South Western railways, operating a shipping service on the Clyde coast was part and parcel of the railway business for the North British. By opening Craigendoran Pier they were in a position to challenge the other two operators for a share of the traffic to the numerous Clyde coast towns. Craigendoran Pier Station was part of Craigendoran Station which also had a platform for West Highland trains. The pier was served by a loop from the Glasgow to Helensburgh line at Craigendoran Station. Competition for passengers on the Clyde coast was fierce at the turn of the twentieth century. The North British provided express trains from Craigendoran Pier directly into Glasgow, but needless to say there was overcapacity and cuts inevitably took place. Services to Craigendoran Pier were taken over by the London and North Eastern Railway Company in 1923 and cut back.

Craigendoran Pier Station, 22 May 1967.

In 1948 all the Clyde coast steamer services came under the ownership of British Railways and were operated as the Caledonian Steam Packet Company Limited. These services were transferred to the Scottish Transport Group in 1969. With the introduction of the 'blue trains' in 1960 electrification came to Craigendoran. In addition to a half-hourly service to and from Glasgow, extra scheduled services were laid on to connect with steamer arrivals and departures. However, by the mid-1960s there were only two arrivals and departures of steamers during the winter months. After the Glasgow September holiday weekend in 1972 the steamer services were withdrawn as well as the special trains that had run in connection with them. The station buildings and pier were demolished in the 1980s, leaving no reminder of Craigendoran's heyday.

Dawsholm – Kirklee (Kelvinside North Junction)

Passenger service withdrawn	1 May 1908	*Station closed*	*Date*
Distance	0.75 miles	Dawsholm	1 May 1908
Company	Caledonian		

Dawsholm was the branch line terminus of one of several lines serving Glasgow Central Low Level Station built by the Caledonian Railway Company in the 1890s. It was an offshoot of the line from Stobcross through Kelvinside, Botanic Gardens and Kirklee stations to Maryhill Central. The station at Dawsholm was situated near the Forth and Clyde Canal and the River Kelvin, and the short branch line even had its own locomotive shed. With the increase in suburban passenger journeys by tramcar the line lost a considerable number of passengers. In 1900 Dawsholm handled 55,000 passenger journeys, but by 1907 this number had fallen to 13,400. The Caledonian decided to close the line the following year, although freight services lasted until 1954.

Dumbarton (East Junction) – Bowling (Dunglass Junction)

Passenger service withdrawn	25 April 1960	*Company*	North British
Distance	3.25 miles		

This line began at a junction just east of Dumbarton Central Station. The route to Bowling was virtually straight and level and passed to the rear of several large whisky bonds. When the Glasgow North 'blue trains' were being planned the decision was made to eventually close one of the two lines from Dumbarton to Bowling. When the closure did come it was the North British line that lost out. Leaving the site of the former Dumbarton East Junction, the line passed through Dumbarton East Station before continuing to Bowling Station which is on the North British line. From there the former North British line to Glasgow is still in use (this required the installation of a new junction at Bowling to link the Caledonian and North British lines). The Caledonian service from Glasgow to Bowling lasted until October 1964 when it was withdrawn as part of the Glasgow Central Low Level line closures. The former North British line route from Bowling to Dumbarton now forms part of the Loch Lomond Cycleway from Glasgow to Balloch.

Elderslie (Canal Junction) – Glasgow (Shields Junction) *

Passenger service withdrawn	10 January 1983	*Stations closed*	*Date*
Distance	8.5 miles	Mosspark	10 January 1983
Company	Glasgow and South Western	Corkerhill	10 January 1983
		Bellahouston Park Halt	1 January 1939
Stations closed	*Date*	Bellahouston	20 September 1954
Crookston	10 January 1983	Shields Road	14 February 1966

On 18 September 1954 class 4 2-6-4T No. 42124 arrives at the newly rebuilt Corkerhill Station with the 2.30 p.m. from St Enoch to Largs.

* Closed stations on this line that were in Renfrewshire were Paisley West, Paisley Canal and Hawkhead.

Crab 2-6-0 No. 42913 passes Bellahouston Station on 3 June 1954 with an evening freight train from College Yard to Dumfries.

The London, Midland and Scottish Railway opened Bellahouston Park Halt in 1925 and the same year created Shields Road by amalgamating the Pollokshields and Shields stations which were reconstructed to form the new station. In April 1991 Strathclyde Passenger Transport Executive reopened the line in part by providing a service from Glasgow Central to Paisley Canal, with stations being reopened or replaced at Paisley Canal, Hawkhead, Crookston, Mosspark West and Corkerhill. At first the frequency provided was hourly, but due to high demand this was increased to half-hourly in November 1992. The Glasgow to Kilmacolm services which at one time ran along this route (and continued in some instances to Greenock's Princess Pier) are no more, but the line survives to this day as one of Scotland's few reopened rail routes. Opened in July 1885, this was known as the Paisley Canal line. Not all stations opened immediately, with Paisley West in use from June 1897, Hawkhead from May 1894 and Crookston from December 1894. Starting at Elderslie Station on the Glasgow and South Western Railway Company's main line from Glasgow St Enoch to Ayr, the line wound its way through the southern suburbs of Paisley and Glasgow before rejoining the same line at Shields Junction. The railway company had great plans for the line which they envisaged would form part of a circular service linking Glasgow, Barrhead and Paisley. This was achieved, but in the event the service didn't last long due to the rapid development of tram routes in the area. A passenger service continued to operate during the First World War, but there was a cutback in the number of stations which remained open to passengers. Hawkhead and Crookston were closed from January 1917 and Bellahouston was only open for workmen's trains. Services were probably reinstated about 1919.

Class 3F 0-6-0 No. 57575 arrives at Shields Road Station with the 5.23 p.m. from Renfrew Fullar Street to St Enoch on 20 April 1955.

Gallowgate – Bellgrove (Sydney Street Junction)

Passenger service withdrawn	1 October 1902	*Company*	Glasgow and South Western
Distance	0.5 miles		

This stretch of line was part of the City of Glasgow Union Railway which was a partnership between the Glasgow and South Western and North British railways. The proposal was that a main line would run from Clyde Junction near St Enoch Station to Springburn, thus linking the main lines operated by the two companies and allowing through traffic. Although the total length was only about 6 ¼ miles there were engineering difficulties and it took eleven years to complete, with Springburn being reached in 1883. The section of line from Bellgrove to Springburn is still in use today, forming part of the route of the Glasgow north suburban services. In 1896 the City of Glasgow Union lines were divided between the Glasgow and South Western and the North British. The former operated local passenger services to Springburn from Govan and Paisley but these were withdrawn in 1902. The partnership between the two companies had allowed through connections between Edinburgh and Ayrshire via Coatbridge and Bellgrove. However, when the Caledonian opened its Central Station in 1897 the improved facilities for passengers changing trains resulted in a loss of passengers and the subsequent withdrawal of these services. Attempts were made to hold on to the traffic by providing a bus link between St Enoch and Queen Street stations but this ceased in 1902. There have been many proposals over the past decade to have this line reinstated in order to provide a link for Ayrshire trains to reach the north side, but all have fallen by the wayside.

Gorbals (Gorbals Junction) – Strathbungo (Strathbungo Junction)

Passenger service withdrawn	27 June 1966	*Station closed*	*Date*
Distance	1.25 miles	Gorbals	1 June 1928
Company	Glasgow, Barrhead and Kilmarnock		

This line was used by trains to and from St Enoch which were travelling south on the Glasgow and South Western line to Kilmarnock and Carlisle. It closed in tandem with St Enoch Station. Only a few trains stopped at the intermediate station at Gorbals, which was near the site of the earlier South Side stations. Before being absorbed by the London, Midland and Scottish on 1 January 1923, the line was jointly operated by the Caledonian and the Glasgow and South Western railways.

Govan – Ibrox (Ibrox East Junction)

Passenger service withdrawn	1 May 1921	*Station closed*	*Date*
Distance	1 mile	Govan	1 May 1921
Company	Glasgow and Paisley Joint		

The line to Govan allowed the shipbuilding industry to be served by trains from other parts of the city such as Springburn in the north. However, when tram services expanded in Glasgow in the early part of the twentieth century the railways could not compete either in terms of frequency or fare levels. Although the main passenger service was withdrawn in May 1921, shipyard workers' services continued until September the following year. The passenger service along the line had previously been withdrawn in July 1885 and reinstated in March 1886; withdrawn again in April 1899 and reinstated in May 1902; and then withdrawn in May 1906 and reinstated in January 1911. The line was owned by the Glasgow and Paisley Joint Railway Company which was a joint company involving the Glasgow and South Western and the Caledonian. Freight services continued to use the line until 1966.

Hyndland – Partick Hill (Partick Junction)

Passenger service withdrawn	5 November 1960	*Station closed*	*Date*
Distance	0.5 miles	Hyndland	5 November 1960
Company	North British		

Hyndland Station, 19 October 1957.

Hyndland Station was opened to passengers in March 1886. It was at the end of a half-mile spur that branched off the suburban line from Glasgow Queen Street Low Level near Partick Hill Station. Hyndland was a terminus for suburban trains from the east of Glasgow including through trains which ran from Edinburgh to Glasgow via Bathgate. The station continued to be used until the electrification of the Glasgow north suburban services in 1960, when it was replaced by the present-day Hyndland station. After closure Hyndland became a maintenance depot for the 'blue trains', serving this function right up until the opening of Yoker Yard in 1989. The track and land were subsequently sold off to form part of a housing development.

Kilsyth – Kirkintilloch (Kelvin Valley West Junction) *

Passenger service withdrawn	6 August 1951	*Station closed*	*Date*
Distance	3.5 miles	Twechar	6 August 1951
Company	North British		

The line from Kilsyth to Kirkintilloch, originally part of the Kelvin Valley Railway, continued westwards towards Torrance and Maryhill Park and provided a passenger service to Glasgow. Opened to passenger traffic in 1878, it provided a service to Glasgow Queen Street, joining the Campsie Branch (from Aberfoyle) at Kirkintilloch and the Edinburgh to Glasgow main line at Lenzie Junction. In 1880 a service ran to Glasgow via Torrance, but this was limited to one train a day due to a dispute between the North British and Kelvin Valley railways regarding receipts for using the latter's line. This situation was resolved when the North British absorbed the Kelvin Valley in 1885. In those days many stations were situated a few miles from the villages they served; such was the case with Twechar Station which was actually at Gavell and was known by that name until 1924.

* The closed station on this line that was in Stirlingshire was Kilsyth.

Kirkintilloch – Lenzie (Campsie Branch Junction)

Passenger service withdrawn	7 September 1964
Distance	1.75 miles
Company	North British

Stations closed	Date
Kirkintilloch	7 September 1964
Back o' Loch Halt	7 September 1964

The line from Kirkintilloch to Lenzie joined the main Edinburgh to Glasgow route via Falkirk at Lenzie and was the first stage of the line that went from Lenzie to Aberfoyle (see also the Aberfoyle – Kirkintilloch section). The station at Back o' Loch Halt was opened by the London and North Eastern Railway and was purely a passenger station. The line was double track to Kirkintilloch and a passenger service from Glasgow Queen Street High Level ran on it. In the few years prior to closure quite a mixture of rolling stock and locomotives were used on the line, ranging from diesel multiple units, to steam locomotives, to North British Class 21 locomotives which had been built just a few miles away at Springburn. The last passenger service on the line provided twelve arrivals and departures with all trains going to or from Glasgow Queen Street High Level. Freight services lasted until 1966.

Kirkintilloch Station, 12 August 1959.

Kirkintilloch (Kelvin Valley East Junction) – Maryhill Park (Kelvin Valley Junction) *

Passenger service withdrawn	2 April 1951
Distance	9.5 miles
Company	North British

Stations closed	*Date*
Summerston	2 April 1951

New diesel multiple units used the Kelvin Valley line during 1958 for driver training and one such working is seen here at closed Summerston Station on a wintry 25 February.

This was the westerly section of the route from Kilsyth to Maryhill. It joined the line from Cowlairs to Westerton at Maryhill Park which is now the terminus of the service from Glasgow Queen Street High Level to Maryhill. The line was built by the Kelvin Valley Railway Company who envisaged it as a trunk route for freight traffic (carrying mainly coal), linking into the North British line at Maryhill. The North British acquired the Kelvin Valley in 1885 and established a direct service from Glasgow Queen Street Low Level to Kilsyth via Partick, Anniesland and Maryhill. Train services were very sparse and very lightly loaded. Summerston Station, for example, served a small cluster of cottages and in the late nineteenth century Bardowie and Balmore were only small villages. In 1948 there was only one train in each direction. The morning train ran from Kilsyth to Glasgow Queen Street Low Level while the teatime return journey began at Bridgeton Central. After closure some specials did visit the line as far as Torrance. The outline of some parts of the line between Balmore and Torrance are still visible today.

* The closed stations on this line that were in Stirlingshire were Torrance, Balmore and Bardowie.

Kirkintilloch (Monklands Junction) – Bothlin Viaduct (Garngaber Exchange Platform)

Passenger service withdrawn	1845		*Station closed*	*Date*
Distance	1 mile		Kirkintilloch	1845
Company	Monkland and Kirkintilloch		Garngaber Exchange Platform	1845

Bothlin Viaduct Station was where the Edinburgh to Glasgow main line passed over the Monkland and Kirkintilloch line. Passengers alighting at the viaduct had to ascend stairs in order to reach the Edinburgh to Glasgow line. The service began in 1844 and only lasted a year. It was horse-drawn and when a rail link was installed from Kirkintilloch to the Edinburgh to Glasgow rail line at Lenzie this service became redundant.

Kirkintilloch Basin – Kirkintilloch (Woodilee Junction)

Passenger service withdrawn	6 March 1846	*Station closed*	*Date*
Distance	0.5 miles	Kirkintilloch Basin	6 March 1846
Company	Monkland and Kirkintilloch		

The station at Kirkintilloch Basin, which opened in 1835, was the Monkland and Kirkintilloch Railway Company's link with the Forth and Clyde Canal. The rail line was built to cater for mineral traffic but a passenger service was also introduced. Initially it continued south towards Airdrie from Kirkintilloch Basin, passing beneath the Edinburgh and Glasgow Railway Company's line at Lenzie. However, when the Monkland and Kirkintilloch established a link from Woodilee Junction to Middlemuir Junction, thereby creating a more convenient Kirkintilloch Station, passenger services to Kirkintilloch Basin were withdrawn, although the station continued to be used for freight traffic until 1966.

Lenzie (Garngaber Junction) – Garnqueen South Junction *

Passenger service withdrawn	10 December 1851
Distance	5 miles
Company	Monkland and Kirkintilloch

The passenger service on what was the Monkland and Kirkintilloch Railway's main line began on 26 December 1844. At first there were four passenger services in each direction between a station at Hallcraig in Airdrie and Garngaber Station on the Edinburgh and Glasgow Railway's main line. Garngaber Station was an exchange platform located about half a mile east of the present-day Lenzie Station. Passengers from Airdrie could change at Garngaber for Glasgow. However, when alternative routes from Airdrie to Glasgow became available the service was withdrawn. Chryston continued to be served by goods trains until 1965 and the siding at what was Garngaber Junction remained in use until October 1963. Today the former railway around Garngaber outside Lenzie has been converted into footpaths which pass under the Edinburgh to Glasgow main line.

* The closed stations on this line that were in Lanarkshire were Garngaber, Chryston and Garnqueen.

London Road – London Road Junction

Passenger service withdrawn	1 November 1895	*Station closed*	*Date*
Distance	1.25 miles	London Road	1 November 1895
Company	Caledonian		

London Road Station was situated in Bridgeton and opened to passenger traffic on 1 April 1879, two years after it had opened to freight traffic. This was the first station in the Bridgeton area and remained in use until the Glasgow Central Low Level line was opened in November 1895. In 1992 the line was still in use as a private freight line.

Maryhill Central (Bellshaugh Junction) – Stobcross (Stobcross Junction)

Passenger service withdrawn	23 November 1959	*Stations closed*	*Date*
Distance	3.75 miles	Kirklee	1 May 1939
Company	Caledonian	Botanic Gardens	6 February 1939
		Kelvin Bridge	4 August 1952

Botanic Gardens Station.

Opened in 1896, this route began just outside Maryhill Central Station where lines diverged. One went across the west end of Glasgow, mainly by tunnels, to Partick while the other went towards the city centre, also via tunnels, until it reached Stobcross where it joined the present-day Glasgow Central Low Level line. There was a tunnel between Kirklee and Kelvin Bridge with an intermediate station at Botanic Gardens which was underground. It was in this tunnel that during the Second World War the Royal train was housed for a few nights for safety reasons. The three intermediate stations were closed during the First World War from January 1917 until June 1919. Although they were permanently closed earlier than the line itself, even after the line closed in 1959 Maryhill Central could still be reached by trains from Glasgow Central Low Level via Partick West. Some remains of the line between the various tunnels can still be seen today.

Class J37 0-6-0 No. 64623 visits closed Kelvin Bridge Station with a railtour composed of goods brake vans, 27 March 1964.

Milngavie:
George Bennie Monorail

In the late 1920s a strange construction began to appear overhead on the section of railway between Milngavie and Hillfoot stations. It consisted of an elevated track and a propeller-driven carriage suspended from a monorail. Invented by Scotsman George Bennie, it was the forerunner to future monorail systems throughout the world. The test track also included a carriage which could travel up to speeds of 120 m.p.h., but within the test track area could only reach 50 m.p.h. An initial run for passengers took place in July 1930 and although this was successful the scheme was too advanced for the period and financial backing was not forthcoming. George Bennie was passionate about his invention but died a bankrupt. His prototype remained in situ until the mid-1950s.

The George Bennie Monorail.

Possil North – Partick West (East and West Junctions)

Passenger service withdrawn	5 October 1964	*Stations closed*	*Date*
Distance	4.75 miles	Possil *	5 October 1964
Company	Caledonian	Maryhill Central	5 October 1964
		Kelvinside	1 July 1942
		Crow Road	6 November 1960
* Renamed Possil North in 1954.		Partick West	5 October 1964

Maryhill Central Station, 12 July 1962.

Class 4 2-6-4T No. 80002 at Crow Road with the 5.19 p.m. service from Rutherglen to Possil on 9 September 1959.

Possil North Station was the northern terminus of a suburban route which wound its way in various directions in a roundabout way to reach Partick where it joined the route to Glasgow's city centre in the east and the shipyards and engineering plants of Clydebank in the west. Although Possil North was the northern terminus most services started at Maryhill Central. In fact there were no services from Maryhill to Possil between 1908 and 1934. Maryhill Central was a fairly large station boasting a through platform in addition to several bay platforms. The next station on the line was Kelvinside, a very grand station built in a cutting to serve the large houses of Glasgow's west end. Although the building was listed for preservation it burnt down a few years ago; some parts remain and are in use as a restaurant. Today it can be viewed from the entrance at Gartnavel General Hospital. From there the line went under the site of the present day Hyndland Station to a station at Crow Road before entering further tunnels to reach the triangular station of Partick West. Depending on which direction trains were going, they would cross over one of two large girder bridges which spanned Dumbarton Road. Following closure the tracks were lifted quickly, although today the entrance to the tunnel between Partick West and Crow Road stations is still visible.

Class 4 2-6-4T No. 42244 at Partick West with the 5.35 p.m. service from Rutherglen to Balloch, 3 August 1960.

St Enoch – Gallowgate Central

Passenger service withdrawn	1 February 1913	*Station closed*	*Date*
Distance	1 mile	Gallowgate	1 October 1902
Company	Glasgow and South Western		

The starting point for this short link was the line that is still used today by freight trains travelling from south of the Clyde to Bellgrove on the north side. Clyde Junction was outside St Enoch Station. Just beyond Gallowgate Station a tunnel was built which emerged near Gallowgate Central. The latter was on the North British branch line from High Street Station to Bridgeton Cross. The Glasgow and South Western hoped to gain additional traffic and began running trains to Bridgeton Cross in 1893. Not a great deal of passenger traffic used the line, however, and it was mainly at rush hours that services were provided. By 1913 the Glasgow and South Western had decided to discontinue its services. After closure the tunnel linking the two lines was sealed. Gallowgate Station was closed when services to Bellgrove and Springburn were withdrawn in 1902.

St Enoch – Saltmarket Junction

Passenger service withdrawn	1 October 1902	*Company*	Glasgow and South Western
Distance	0.25 miles		

St Enoch Station was at the apex of a triangle with most trains arriving there from the south of Glasgow. Some services went into St Enoch and out again before continuing their journey to either Springburn via Bellgrove or Bridgeton via Gallowgate Central. These trains originated in Paisley and Govan. When services to Springburn were withdrawn in 1902 the last passenger service over this short spur was also withdrawn. The line remained in use until St Enoch closed in 1966, mainly for the stabling of locomotives and rolling stock.

St Enoch – Shields (Shields Junction)

Passenger service withdrawn	27 June 1966	*Stations closed*	*Date*
Distance	1.75 miles	St Enoch	27 June 1966
Company	Glasgow and South Western	Main Street	1 October 1900
		Cumberland Street *	14 February 1966

St Enoch Station.

* Known as Eglinton Street until 1924.

Standard class 4 2-6-0 No. 76093 at
St Enoch Station on 19 April 1965.

St Enoch Station in Glasgow's city centre was opened on 17 October 1876 by the Prince and Princess of Wales. Owned at first by the City of Glasgow Union Railway Company, the station and associated lines were soon acquired by the Glasgow and South Western Railway Company who established its headquarters at the station. Like Glasgow Central Station, a hotel was built within the station and at that time this was reputed to be the largest hotel owned by any railway company in Scotland. The station was a very grand affair and its construction and size compared very favourably with many others south of the border. The majority of services from Ayrshire terminated at St Enoch although for a limited period some local services ran onwards to Bridgeton and Springburn. In the early 1960s St Enoch handled trains to Ayr, Kilmarnock, East Kilbride, Stranraer, Beith and Barrhead as well as through services to London St Pancras which went via the Glasgow and South Western line to Carlisle, the Settle and Carlisle line to Leeds and south to London. The intermediate stations at Main Street and Cumberland Street were very close to each other. Although Main Street in the Gorbals closed in 1900, Cumberland Street remained open until February 1966. The façade of Cumberland Street Station survives to this day as a listed building. After St Enoch closed it was used as a car park for several years before being demolished to make way for the St Enoch shopping centre. Today, arches which formed the approach to St Enoch can still be seen near Glasgow Cross where they are used by small firms.

An Intercity diesel multiple unit, forming the 12.06 p.m. from Largs to St Enoch, passes Cumberland Street Station on 11 February 1966.

St Rollox – Milton Junction

Passenger service withdrawn	1 November 1849	*Station closed*	*Date*
Distance	2.25 miles	St Rollox (first)	1 November 1849
Company	Caledonian		

When the line to Buchanan Street Station was opened the route from Milton Junction was closed to passenger traffic. It had been hoped to extend the line to Buchanan Street in the city centre, but the considerable cost and amount of work required resulted in an alternative route being sought. The line continued to Port Dundas and remained open for freight traffic until 1979.

Shettleston (Shettleston Junction) – Bothwell *

Passenger service withdrawn	4 July 1955	*Stations closed*	*Date*
Distance	5.25 miles	Mount Vernon North	4 July 1955
Company	North British	Broomhouse	24 September 1927
		Calderpark Halt for the Zoo	4 July 1955

Opened on 1 April 1878, this was an attempt by the North British Railway to make an inroad into the territory of one of its rivals – the Caledonian Railway. The line originally extended to Hamilton but closed in 1952 due to the dangerous state of a viaduct between Bothwell and Hamilton. Train services ran from Hyndland via Glasgow Queen Street Low Level. Passenger levels were never very high due to the close proximity of other railway lines and the service offered was generally very sparse.

* Stations on this line that were in Lanarkshire were Maryville, Uddingston West, Uddingston East and Bothwell.

Singer Works Platform – Singer Junction

Passenger service withdrawn	8 May 1967	Station closed	*Date*
Distance	0.5 miles	Singer Works Platform	8 May 1967
Company	North British		

Singer Works Platform.

This extensive works platform was built to serve the vast complex belonging to the Singer Manufacturing Company of New Jersey. Built in 1883, the 46 acre site needed a large workforce which could not be found within the Clydebank area where the factory was located. Every day a vast influx of trains arrived from east and west of Clydebank and converged on the Singer works. For example, on a weekday morning between 6 a.m. and 7 a.m. about fourteen workers' trains would arrive. Singer Works Platform had about eight platforms to accommodate the workers' trains. When the north side suburban services were electrified in 1960 the Singer Platform branch was too, although some trains were still steam operated as they ran to Springburn via Westerton and Maryhill. This particular service was withdrawn in March 1964. Like many manufacturing industries a run-down took place in the 1960s and it was eventually decided that there was no need for such a large complex. Today Singer's name lives on as the present Singer Station on the line from Glasgow to Helensburgh and is one of the few stations in Britain named after a manufacturing company. Today nothing remains of the Singer factory or the vast works platform complex.

Ivatt Mogul No. 43134 and V3s Nos. 67648, 67625 and 67618 at the Singer terminal platforms with workers' trains for Glasgow, 28 August 1956.

South Side – Gushetfaulds Junction

Passenger service withdrawn	1 July 1879	*Station closed*	*Date*
Distance	0.5 miles	South Side	1 July 1879
Company	Caledonian		

South Side was one of two stations of the same name which sat side by side but were owned by different companies. The other one belonged to the Glasgow, Barrhead and Kilmarnock Joint Railway Company. The Caledonian station served trains coming from Lanarkshire and was built before the Clyde was crossed by any railway and also before the construction of Glasgow's famous terminal stations – Central and St Enoch. The station at South Side was a primitive wooden structure which was rebuilt in the 1850s. Although the rebuilding resulted in quite an impressive new station this too was subsequently demolished in order to link lines when the Clyde was being crossed. Platform facilities did, however, remain until the station was closed in 1879.

South Side – Langside Junction

Passenger service withdrawn	1 October 1877	*Station closed*	*Date*
Distance	0.5 miles	South Side	1 October 1877
Company	Glasgow, Barrhead and Kilmarnock Joint		

This was the other South Side station and stood next to the Caledonian Railway's station of the same name. It consisted of a bay platform and was very basic, serving trains coming from the south-west of Glasgow. It continued to be used until the new stations at Central and St Enoch were available.

Speirsbridge – Kennishead

Passenger service withdrawn	1 May 1849	*Station closed*	*Date*
Distance	1 mile	Speirsbridge	1 May 1849
Company	Glasgow, Barrhead and Neilston		

Opened in 1848, this was one of the first attempts to introduce a suburban service to the outskirts of Glasgow. Traffic levels were low and the passenger service was withdrawn after only six months. Freight services along the branch lasted until September 1941.

Whiteinch Victoria Park – Jordanhill (Whiteinch West Junction)

Passenger service withdrawn	2 April 1951	*Station closed*	*Date*
Distance	0.75 miles	Whiteinch Victoria Park	2 April 1951
Company	North British		

This short branch line was one of the termini which the North British used for its suburban services. The line left the present-day Hyndland to Dalmuir via Yoker route at a junction to the east of Jordanhill Station and as the name implies the station was near Victoria Park. Whiteinch was also served by the Caledonian on its service from Glasgow Central Low Level which was generally considered to be a more convenient route. After the withdrawal of passenger services in 1951 the line was retained for freight traffic until the mid-1960s and was used extensively by works trains during the electrification of the Glasgow north suburban services in the late 1950s.

Closed passenger stations on lines still open to passenger services

Line/Service	**Bellgrove – Springburn**	*Line/Service*	**Drumgelloch – Helensburgh Central via Singer** *
Station	*Date of closure*		
Garngad *	1 March 1910	* Known as Blochairn until 1885.	

Parkhead Station, looking east, 30 August 1955.

Line/Service   **Drumgelloch – Helensburgh Central via Singer ***
(continued)

Station closed	Date
Parkhead North **	19 September 1955
Finnieston	1 January 1917

Station closed	Date
Yorkhill ***	1 April 1921
Partick Hill ****	17 December 1979
Kilbowie	3 November 1907
Dalmuir (first)	17 May 1897
Bowling (first)	31 May 1858

Class B1 4-6-0s Nos. 61099 and 61081 run into Partick Hill Station with a Glasgow autumn holiday excursion from Balloch to Edinburgh Waverley on 26 September 1960.

* Closed station on this line that were in Lanarkshire were Cairnhill Bridge and Bargeddie.
** Known as Parkhead until 30 June 1952.

*** Closed from 1 January 1917 until 1 February 1919.
**** Known as Partick until 28 February 1953.

Line/Service	**Fort William – Craigendoran (Junction) ***	Station closed	Date

| | | | Shandon | 15 June 1964 |

Station closed	Date
Inveruglas Platform **	c.1948
Glen Douglas Halt	15 June 1964
Whistlefield Halt ***	15 June 1964

Station closed	Date
Shandon	15 June 1964
Faslane Platform ****	c.1949
Rhu *****	15 June 1964
Craigendoran (West Highland Station)	15 June 1964

Glen Douglas Halt on 28 January 1961 with a railbus on the 11.40 a.m. run from Craigendoran to Arrochar and Tarbet Station.

* The closed station on this line that was in Inverness-shire was Fersit Halt. The closed station in Argyll was Gorton. The closed station in Perthshire was Glen Falloch Platform.
** Closed after completion of hydroelectric scheme.

*** Known as Whistlefield until 13 June 1960.
**** Closed after completion of hydroelectric scheme.
***** Closed from 9 January 1956 until 4 April 1960.

Line/Service

**Glasgow (Queen Street) – Edinburgh
via Falkirk High ***

Station closed
Cowlairs
Dullatur

Date
7 September 1964
5 June 1967

**A2 Pacific No. 60530, 'Sayajirao', passes Cowlairs Station with the noon
express from Queen Street to Edinburgh Waverley on 21 October 1955.**

* Closed stations on this line that were in Stirlingshire were Castlecary, Upper Greenhill, Greenhill and Bonnybridge High.
Closed stations in the Lothians were Manuel, Philipstoun, Winchburgh, Ratho, Gogar and Saughton.

Line/Service	**Gretna Junction – Glasgow via Carstairs ***	Station closed	Date
		Rutherglen (second)	5 November 1979
Station closed	Date	Gushetfaulds **	1 May 1907
Rutherglen (first)	31 March 1879	Eglinton Street	1 February 1965

Royal Scot 4-6-0 No. 46160, 'Queen Victoria's Rifleman', passes Rutherglen with a 5.53 p.m. autumn holiday special from Glasgow Central to Blackpool, 25 September 1964.

* Closed stations on this line that were in Dumfriesshire were Kirkpatrick, Kirtlebridge, Ecclefechan, Nethercleugh, Dinwoodie, Whamphray, Beattock. Closed stations in Lanarkshire were Elvanfoot, Crawford, Abington, Lamington, Symington (first), Symington (second), Thankerton, Cleghorn, Braidwood, Law Junction, Wishaw South, Flemington, Motherwell (first), Fallside and Newton (first).

** Known as Cathcart Road until 1 July 1886.

Eglinton Street Station on 9 May 1964 with a diesel multiple unit forming the 7.55 a.m. service from Carstairs to Glasgow Central.

Line/Service	**Gretna Junction – Glasgow via Dumfries ***	*Station closed*	*Date*
		Strathbungo	28 May 1962
		Bridge Street	1 March 1905

* Closed stations on this line that were in Dumfriesshire were Gretna Green, Rigg, Eastriggs, Cummertrees, Ruthwell, Racks, Dumfries (first), Dumfries (second), Holywood, Auldgirth, Closeburn, Thornhill, Carronbridge and Sanquhar. Closed stations in Ayrshire were New Cumnock, Cumnock, Auchinleck, Mauchline, Hurlford, Kilmaurs, Stewarton, Dunlop and Lugton. Closed stations in Renfrewshire were Uplawmoor, Neilston Low and Neilston (first).

Black Five No. 44992 at Strathbungo on 26 May 1962 with the 5.38 p.m. service from St Enoch to Kilmarnock, the last train to call before closure of the station.

Line/Service	Rutherglen Junction – Whifflet *	Station closed	Date
		Mount Vernon **	16 August 1943
		Baillieston **	5 October 1964

* The closed station on this line that was in Lanarkshire was Langloan.

** Reopened 4 October 1993.

Line/Service	**Springburn – Cumbernauld ***	*Station closed*	*Date*
		Robroyston	11 June 1956

* Closed stations on this line that were in Lanarkshire were Stepps, Garnkirk, Gartcosh and Glenboig.

Line/Service	**Westerton (Knightswood North Junction) – Cowlairs**	*Station closed*	*Date*
		Maryhill Park *	2 October 1961
		Lochburn	1 January 1917
		Possilpark **	1 January 1917

J37 0-6-0 No. 64633 calls at Maryhill Park Station with the Saturday 12.10 p.m. workers' train from Singer to Duke Street, 8 April 1961.

* Closed from 2 April 1951 until 19 December 1960. Known as Maryhill until 15 September 1952. Reopened as Maryhill on 6 December 1993.

** Reopened as Possilpark and Parkhouse on 6 December 1993.